Sanity Went on Vacation

<u>Sanity Went on Vacation</u>

To Karen,
Treasure
Yourself

[signature]

12/00

Ken Siegmann

The Bent Eagle Press
Sunnyvale, CA
ISBN 0-9677988-0-9

The Bent Eagle Press
595 Balsam Ave.
Sunnyvale, CA 94086

Internet e-mail: siegmann@best.com

Also by Ken Siegmann:
"The Second Coming and Other Poems" (Toth Press)
ISBN 0-9646610-3-9

Acknowledgements

Moondance: "George"
Poetic Express: "Baby Changing"
Baker Street Irregular: "Where Are You Now, Jack?"
Left Hand Maps: "Duke"
The Montserrat Review: "Remembering Frank and my
Father"
Will Work for Peace: "The Second Coming"

Printed in Canada

Editor: Layne Russell
Layout and design: Jamyang Yonten
Cover Art: Lynn Grant

CONTENTS

For my brother Richard
the best man I know

For it is important that awake people be awake

– William Stafford

SUBURBIA

I can't write in the city.
Put me in the woods, and the words
flow like torrential rain
into a shot glass.

I may be lying about this.
After all, I live in the city, or at least
in suburbia, where trees punctuate the asphalt
and the saltbox houses and the wires overhead.

I sell words for a living. They're expensive.
I write to save my life. It's worth saving.

I can't write in the city.
I do it anyway.
It's just that the lodgepole pine in Yosemite
speaks louder and more gently
than the magnolia in my back yard.
I love them both.

MEADOW AT JIKOJI

Green dragonfly clings to a dandelion stalk
like I cling to serenity.

I'm surrounded by small black flies, buzzing
around this clearing of gold grass and purple flowers.

After all, I'm in their space, listening
to birds, gazing at trees, wondering.

A small redwood shrine sits atop a pedestal
in the woods, an impressionistic Buddha,

not quite a Buddha, though it implies one.
Fresh purple flowers in a jar and a picture

of a young boy smiling. I wonder who he is.
Maybe he's dead. Someone grieves somewhere.

My assumptions don't matter, only the breeze,
the black butterfly with orange tipped wings.

Bird calls tweedle de deet, deet, deet and the warm buzz
of the woods. Maybe I'll just sit here forever.

GEORGE

Romance is forever
So he is not alone
Gazes through the gentle flames of slender candles
White linen, a table for two
The simple elegance of an eighty-year love affair.
Til death do they part
They have not parted
He cannot see her, nor go on without her
She is with him still
In silence he feels her voice
Oh for the love of Grace
A life of love and music
Art and philosophy
Children and laughter
Rewriting Shakespeare
"Then ten times happy we..."

REMEMBERING FRANK AND MY FATHER

for Gene Siegmann

My father taught us about
Frank Sinatra,
driving down the highway

in his spanking new white 1965 Buick,
with the white metal dashboard
and red leather seats,

playing the radio, he would sing
It Happened in Monterey,
between rants and raves
about the Nelson Riddle arrangements.
I thought he sounded like Frank.

My brother carried the tune
at age seven, insisting he sounded
like Ol' Blue Eyes,
singing *You Make Me Feel So Young*
in our living room in his pajamas.
His voice hadn't even cracked yet.

I didn't talk to my father for years
and after we reconciled

I would buy Frank Sinatra
records when I saw them at
garage sales or in used record bins
and take them to him.

I remember looking for
These Foolish Things
for years after

I heard Art Pepper play it.
I knew there was only one
recording that mattered.
I found it on an album
simply called
The Voice,
with young Frank
on the musty cover.

It smelled the way
old records used to smell
before CD's came out with
clean plastic covers.
The vinyl was perfect
as a baritone crooner.

My father loved it, even though
he had lost his hearing by then.

I think of my father,
often with little tenderness.

But today, after
the Chairman of the Board
has gone and only
the music remains

I am reminded again
how all too seldom
I recognize .
the many gifts he gave me.

MILES

The first thing I noticed was the room
started to feel like velvet and a subtle smoothness
entered the air. I wanted to lean back in my chair
and absorb the moment. But I was sitting on a bar stool

in a dimly lit New York basement tavern,
drinking creamy, dark drafts of Guinness Stout. The deep, rich
brew was smooth and slightly bitter. It was raining outside.
I didn't know I was hearing Miles Davis for the first time.

I didn't know I would sell my collection of rock n' roll
records and buy every Miles record I could find.
I didn't know I would fall in love with the one
instrument it took me the longest time to appreciate.

I didn't know I would become a poet.
Twenty years later I feel the same warmth in my belly
when a poem by Billy Collins reminds me of the days
before compact disks when I would sit on the floor

in front of the turntable, move the tone arm back again
and again and again and listen to All Blues
over and over. It's never over. Three thousand
jazz records later, I still think of Miles when I feel the muse.

Now I seek inspiration in book stores. In my post-yuppy days
I sit in coffee houses, sip Cafe Mochas and listen to poetry.
I am grateful for the unending melodies in a life where
jazz and poetry are indistinguishable.

SANITY WENT ON VACATION

Sanity went on vacation.
He hopped a flight to Cabo San Lucas
with a maxed-out credit card. Checked into
a hotel he couldn't afford and went out
to pick up chicks on the beach.

Sanity thought of calling his wife,
but he was on vacation, so
he didn't give a shit. Chugged another
beer, knocked back another shot
of gold tequila – only the best –
ate the worm at the bottom of the bottle,

crawled inside where he felt safe,
rolled a joint and stayed there
waiting for the next disaster.

Sanity got depressed and wondered
what his life would become, obsessed
over what to do next, who to call,
where to go, the mistakes he made,
the mistakes he would make,
the people he's hurt,
though he never met them.

He felt like a fuck-up.

Sanity wondered how
long this vacation
would take before he got to go
back to work. He wanted to go to
an AA meeting. But he didn't –
too much like work.

He wanted to commit suicide.

Sanity went back to the bar
ordered another round. Got belligerent
with the bar tender, got thrown out
onto the dark street, got into a fight,
beat himself up, wandered among
the closed shops, peered into windows

at things he could not have,
feelings he could not feel,
people he could not love,
opportunities he missed.

He hated himself.

Sanity did the same thing
day after day after day.
He couldn't understand why
the results were always the same.

Sanity remembered it was time
to go. It felt like work. He packed his bags, stole
the towels and sheets from his hotel room,
left without settling the bill,
stiffed the cab driver on the way to the airport.
He started to feel better on the plane,
actually smiled at a small child,

got off the plane in San Francisco,
took a cab to his office,
called his wife,
settled back to work.
Everything will be OK.

BABY CHANGING

The sign on the bathroom wall reads
"Baby Changing Station."
And I'm thinking,
what do they change into – adults maybe?
Is this where babies change
from the innocence of helplessness
to the preoccupied beasts
the rest of us have become?

Or maybe they're changing stations,
you know, like from
Port Authority Terminal to Grand Central Station,
so they can leave the city and go to the country
and find themselves in a rural setting
where the schools are better
and there's less crime in the streets
and open space isn't a political issue
because there's lots of it
and they can play in the meadows
without venturing far from home.

Or maybe they're changing stations
from holder of cuteness and warmth for society
to convenient scapegoats for conservatives
who believe doing away with welfare
will put an end to their existence out of wedlock,
as if that will solve anything.

Or maybe it's where parents change
their diapers, and I just think too much.

BUDDHA SIPS GREEN TEA

Buddha sips green tea with both hands
from a small round cup. He ponders
the warmth in his palms, inhales the soothing
vapors. He sits on a round vinyl stool

hunched over a white, speckled formica
counter of a greasy luncheonette
in a working-class neighborhood
in San Francisco. He ponders

a homeless alcoholic who slouches
on the next stool, drooling
into his coffee, huddled in his dingy
grey overcoat. It matches his scraggly beard.

Buddha sips green tea. Two Generation Xers
wearing black leather and spiked bracelets,
black leather boots, nose rings, purple hair
hassle the homeless drunk, call him names.

The drunk doesn't seem to notice. Buddha stills
their hearts with a single glance, awakens their
compassion, just as they open their mouths to razz
Buddha about his top-knot. There's nothing

like sudden enlightenment to silence rowdy kids.
Buddha stares into his soft green tea, like it is
the only vessel in the universe, sips slowly.
The homeless drunk puts his head on the bar,

begins to snore. Buddha feels like nodding,
takes another sip of tea, waits for the old
man to awaken and continue his teachings.
Buddha sips green tea.

MEDITATION

It's enough to make a grown man
blow up his own TV.
                    -- John Prine

I blew up the television,
stopped reading the newspaper.
My mind still makes a lot of noise.
I blew my mind in the 60s.

It didn't help.

Years later, after sobriety,
my mind still drifts me out of reality.

Now I practice Vipassana meditation.
I sit every morning with my back straight,
my eyes closed. I focus on my breath
while my mind swings like a pendulum.

I breathe and watch.

I blew up the television.
It couldn't hurt.

WHERE ARE YOU NOW, JACK?

All things
Are empty
And in essence
Eternal
                    – Jack Kerouac

I'm as you imagine,
sitting Zen on the Matterhorn
with Gary Snyder, contemplating
Charlie Parker and Neil Cassady.
I'm pouring port from a jug at your
favorite poetry reading.

I'm far out in time and space,
being the Bodisattva, the Buddha,

          don't you get it,

playing yabyum with princess
and Allen Ginsberg. I'm sitting
at my desk, proving that I am

a neanderthal with a typewriter
my fingers on the keys typing madness,
proving it, proving it!

I drank myself to death on purpose.
It was stupendous!

Fuck you if you think
I'm some sort of tragic figure.
Fuck you if you think
I died in pain. It was bliss,

total bliss. I am the Bodhisattva.
I am the Buddha. I am Han-shan
and Shih-te and every Zen lunatic
you ever imagined.

> It's easy.
> It's tragic
> > like life.

I wrote Mexico City Blues as a scam.
They don't play the blues
in Mexico City. I heard the blues
on a dusty side street
where an old woman preached Jesus
and pounded tortillas.

I waited for the words and they always came,
always, that's the beauty of it. You know

they held that symposium
about me at New York University.
None of those cats ever

woke up drunk on the floor
all woebegone and goopy, groaning
in a skid row hotel in the Mission district
and missed their ride and had to hitch hike
with a rucksack
to Big Sur and got lost in the woods
in the dark with the shakes
because I ran out of port and money. I was trying

to find Ferlinghetti's house in Big Sur
because he said I could stay as long as I wanted
if I speed-typed his manuscript.

None of them ever shouted haiku
from the high, dry Sierra
with Japhy Ryder and Morley,
or spent the summer, the
whole summer, sitting

Zen alone
      on a mountain
            getting paid for it.

Where am I now? I'm standing
in my gi on the front cover of that book you paid $30 for
because you wanted to know what the Dharma really is.

I have become the emptiness you crave.
I have become the emptiness I craved.
It's real, man. Don't worry about it.

URBANISMA

1

I saw a woman smoking two cigars
while Peruvian musicians
played outside Burger King.

Yuppies and street people,
addicts and normals,
white balloons, dancing children
and a woman smoking two cigars.

Just another night
on the town.

2

Three homeless men
argue under the awning of a flower shop.
"We already asked him," says
the one with the long beard.
I smile and shrug.
I know these men.
Today, I have no loose change in my pockets.

At least I'm not ignoring them.

3

Where do you live, man?
My son and I set up a tent down by Stevens Creek,
can I wash your car window?
Reaching into my pocket, I produce $1.34.
It's all I have on me. Put it in his outstretched hand.
I may never have to clean that window again.

4

They barely spoke over dinner
in an expensive restaurant
he at 400 pounds, she an anorexic.

They didn't look at each other.
He held his thick glasses in his hand
so she appeared

as a watercolor haze
though he could see well enough
to eye the waitress.

5

"I see two challenges and one wish,"
he said as they left the hardware store. "And
you can turn one of the wishes
into a challenge." She just looked at him.
They walked on.

The store is called "Restoration Hardware."
It sells upscale door knobs and hardwood furniture
for people who wear leather pants
and vote Democratic and complain
about the homeless.

Palo Alto wouldn't dare
have a regular hardware store that sells screw drivers
right there on University Avenue.

6

Bobbi walks by dressed like an eggplant
in her purple rain coat. She clutches
four roles of Christmas wrapping paper she got
on sale. It's the day after Christmas.

7

A woman leaves the hardware store with a mop.
She looks purposeful. Gets to the end of the block,
pauses,
turns around and walks back to the hardware store.
Even the gentry get confused.

8

Anonymous in the city, I look
for familiar faces in book stores.
Of course, they all look familiar.

I remember Oneonta, New York,
population 7,000, surrounded
by nothing. I knew everyone.

9

I am reminded once again, I
live in the city. It's not
that I don't like it here.

The two trees
in my front yard and in my back yard
don't speak loud enough.

JULIA PFEIFER STATE BEACH

I don't write poems
about beaches
about turquoise waves
of serenity crashing
into white foam.

I don't write poems
about caves and coves
where water breathes
gently up and down
gently up and down.

I don't write poems
about sea otters
and kelp
miracles in mist
driftwood in sand.

I don't write poems
about the turbulent doorway
to other lands
filled with foam and sea and waves
becoming itself, becoming me.

I don't spend enough time here.

JAZZBEAUX

for Al "Jazzbeaux" Collins

Al was selling Frog Juice
on the radio at 2 a.m.
I was driving a cab in New York,
contemplating what it was like
to drive all night
without a destination.

Al played Count Basie a lot,
said *mah man* a lot
talked purple jazz
occasionally played Duke Ellington.

Years later, I found Al
in San Francisco,
called him on the phone
to talk about those lonely nights
behind the wheel.
        Mah man, he said, and told me
about the time he drove
his red Porche up the hill
in Elmsford.

Once I caught Al calling
the secret studio
to talk about jazz and bebop
and things purple. I called him
at midnight to tell him
Art Pepper had died.
        Mah man, he said, *I'm goin.'*
        Maybe I'll catch you around sometime.

ART PEPPER

I heard you moaning
through your alto saxophone,
like the warm rush of heroin
after a long night on the road.

And I wondered about that airy tone,
and I wondered about *Patricia*,
and I wondered why the Straight Life
had to be so hard -- hard as the tone

of your last years, when you recorded
For Lauri, Mambo de la Pinta and Chris' Blues.
You changed me, you know, the way Miles did.
I still weep when I think about that night

in Berkeley when you brought us to our knees
with a single line and Carl Burnette played
like clockwork and I saw you warming up
your clarinet in the dressing room.

One night I thought I heard
a lone wolf baying at the moon.
It was you, playing *Goodbye*, probably not
the way Benny Goodman intended it.

And I wondered why the Straight Life
had to be so hard, and remembered
how the softness of your tone
blended with the strings when you played

Blues in the Night.

McCoy Tyner

Little Darling
You ruined it.
Nobody could play it like you did
that night in the jazz club that served sushi.
Nobody would dare.

Your fingers blurred on the keys,
an orchestra in your hands.
You scared me.

God I thought
if he plays any better
he just might kill us.

Here's That Rainy Day
The house moans.
Lift us up. We weep.

There's a woman sitting next to me
nineteen or so.
Her music appreciation teacher sent her here
to experience jazz.

"Is this guy famous?" she asks,
just before you sit down.
"Is he the real thing, I mean real jazz?"

It doesn't get more real than this.
Now put down that notebook and open your mind
before McCoy blows your brains out.

Sweat drips on the keys.
I'm on my knees
too intense
too intense

Jazz floats me out of my chair
scours the inside of my head
opens my heart
caresses my soul like a cool breeze.

Seeing Keith Jarrett

The piano moans,
or maybe it's the piano player,
or maybe it's me. I'm floating

above rows of seats, filled
with rapt faces. The piano
soft as feathers on velvet

When I fall in love...

The piano moans,
The drummer is a metronome,
a bass so deep

you could splunk your way
down a minor scale.

...it will be forever...

This is the soul of jazz.
This is sweetness.
This is the only moment.

Black and white keys dance
in my head. My fingers
are hammers that strike

the taut strings of melody
and dissonance.

My funny valentine...

The piano moans.
or maybe it's the piano player,
or maybe it's me.

...sweet, comic valentine...

I know I'll never recover,
at least I hope not,

...you make me smile with my heart...

NOT A WORD

> *Cat no say I am cat.*
> *Cat just say meow.*
> -- Zen Master Seung Sahn Soen-sa

Imagine
a world
without
words.

Would
there still
be chatter
in my
head?
What
would
it sound
like?

How would
anyone ever
run for office,
sell cigarettes
to kids and
deny it? Would
we have

buildings
and streets
and cars,
computers and
men in blue
suits, white
shirts, red ties
and black
shoes with

briefcases?

Would we
moan during
orgasm?
What would
we do with
the telephones
and radios?
Would we
bring back
silent
movies?
Would we

be closer to God,
nature, trees,
the desert,
the sea,
clouds
blue sky?
Would we
be like cats,
purring,
eating,
sleeping,
an occasional
meow?

Would music
be improvisational?
What would
the pundits do?

I imagine
Nirvana
as silence
like snow

drifting
over the prairie,
like eagles
soaring and
egrets softly
touching the
brown earth,
where even
the mockingbird
is content
to merely
listen.

HIKING HAIKU

Woods quiet my mind
the way foamy ocean waves
smooth the sandy beach.

Forgotten Almost

The night of the electrical storm
on Hopi Mesa, we huddled dry in our tent
in a muddy parking lot.
Mother thundered and wept.

In a tent on a mesa three thousand feet
above the desert. Mother raged outside
and a stray dog crouched under a tree,
next to the shelter, waiting silently.

The next day I wondered,
what are we doing here?

When I saw the Kachina in the window,
I knew why we had come to this holy land
where the Hopi have lived for three thousand years.

We ate blue corn pancakes at the inn on Third Mesa,
listened to a local guide tell a local reporter
the Hopi know the white man will destroy the mother
and the Hopi will protect her as best they can.

After all, he said,
isn't that why men built rockets?
To go into space and find a new home
when they are done with this one?

And I thought of the big corporation
that built its plant in the Arizona desert
where it would consume the aquifer
in just 25 years. Poured more syrup
on my gritty blue pancakes

while the guide explained why
the Hopi don't want another corporation
to mine Uranium from their land.

The Kachina was tall, like the corn stalk
carved into her side. The sun rose in her
face, while Kokopelli danced and played,
and the desert below drifted from deep
blue to orange to yellow sand, pocked with
green shrubs. I thought of the mesa dwellers

dry farming the earth below, praying and sweating
in Kivas. I thought of Kachinas walking into
snow-capped mountains, carrying baskets
of prayers. I thought of dances, forbidden
to the white man who disrespected the land,
disrespected the Hopi, disrespected the mother.

I thought of thunder and wind that
whipped the sides of our tent in the mud,
of the raging mother. I felt my feet planted
firmly on the ground. I felt the sun warm my
back, bake the desert, coax corn from the land.

I still see the Kachina from time to time.
I tell friends about the night we spent
in the tent, in the storm on Third Mesa.
I talk about the dog who ate the beef jerky we threw away,
about driving through the Arizona desert.

I had forgotten, almost, about the mystical moment
when the Kachina appeared and I felt rooted to the earth.

PANTHER MEADOW

I want to weep,
to peer between thin blades of
green grass, to seep into the sacred
spring that feeds Panther Meadow.

The meadow listens
for an echo no one can hear
unless absolutely at one
with small red buds,

yellow flowers and
the holy spirit
that holds the sacred ground.
I know this place as well
as I know myself. It holds

the great mystery in an open
palm. Desire is meaningless.
Anger is meaningless. Longing
for the great OM is also meaningless.
What do we want that is not God?

What do we ache for that is not
the aching of the spirit for compassion?
This alpine meadow at the top of
the tree line holds the answer
and speaks silently.

PURPLE HEART FLUTE

He brought the flute to his lips,
breathed a song
from his
opening heart.

Cool water
caressed smooth stones
in a mountain stream,
joined a river
floated effortlessly
to the open sea.

Kachinas carried baskets
of prayers into drifting
clouds on mountain tops.

A gentle breeze
touched his face.

He closed his eyes,
swayed to the deep,
rich tone that soothed
his belly, whispered his thoughts
away, settled his spirit.

Miles later,
he still hears
a woody echo.

ROUTE 66 ARIZONA

for Bobby Troupe

Elvira Hill can name everyone who lives
in Hackberry, Arizona. And she does
when I ask, "How many people live
in Hackberry?"

We stopped for gas, Ed and me, once we realized
we weren't going to make it

to the Grand Canyon by sunset. We were stoned,
getting our kicks
at the gas pump
with the whirligig on top, like the ones
I'd seen in books.

The pool table listed. Ninety-five
and dry outside. We played pool, drank
hot brown coffee from styrofoam cups,
inspected dusty cans of Spam,
quizzed Elvira over the noisy air conditioner.
She was affable enough,

even came outside to take our picture
by the gas pumps. Big smiles and a rented
white 1983 Toyota Tercel caught in time.

Years later, midway between Kingman and Seligman,
the store is boarded up, whirligigs are gone,
a big hole where gas tanks used to be. Warm desert
wind and sand blow while I peel the sign
off the window to prove
more than ghosts once lived here.

Peering through the window, the pool table still lists,
at least I like to think so.
Where's Ed? Where's Elvira? If everything
is impermanent, like Buddha said,
why did I come back to this place?

Years later, I sit alone and listen
to my favorite dead Canadian folk musician
and write a poem. In my mind's eye, sand

covers the Hackberry General Store, the woman
with the bouffant hairdo, the white Cadillac with fins,
the neon pink flamingo and the red bandanna
I tied to the door.

FIVE CANOE HAIKU

flat water canoe
drifts among green lily pads
paddles knock and drip

birds on the island
silhouette in orange sun
waves lap tranquil shore

loon calls only once
canoe passes slowly by
roots in the water

stars on the still lake
Milky Way above at peace
loon in the distance

blue sky flat water
canoeing in the desert
warm sun soothes my back

FLICKERING LIGHT

The flickering light is an airplane
against purple clouds at sunset.
I want to think it's something else.

Perhaps it's God
piercing through the night.
Perhaps it's a UFO coming to take me away, ha ha.

Perhaps the crickets
are really singing
Ode to Joy.

So What

for Miles Davis

Passionate intensity
the sweetness of your tone,
soft and sweet
and cool and blue.

Carry me back
to the place where jazz
and my soul sing
soft and sweet

and cool and blue.
You weave
velvet into burlap
In a Silent Way.

It's *All Blues*
and hard bop.
You gave me
Sketches of Spain,

Straight no Chaser
and I'll never be the same.
You were the ultimate
motherfucker

soft rage that weeps
into a space so deep
nobody but nobody
could touch you.

JOHN COLTRANE

Coltrane
Soultrane on the A Trane
Blue Trane

Sputtering melodic, violent
harmonic, sweet as love, deep
as the weeping child

grown to a man who moans
with a reed in his mouth and
a saxophone growing out of his face.

DUKE

In my Solitude I contemplate
Edward Kennedy Ellington
(even your name swings)
with the reverence of a Samurai on his knees
before the master.
I could *Take the A Train*
to Harlem itself and still not
know the joy of the Piano Player.

In a Sentimental Mood,
you soothe me like a sacred
clarinet, or maybe a robust tenor
moaning *In a Mellow Tone.*

If Billy Strayhorn were Messiah,
you'd be God. We'll settle for
your humble Dukeness, lighting the *Sweet St. Louis* sky
with an orchestra so fine
Gabriel would put down his horn, angels
would hang up their harps, monks would cease to chant
the holy Om and the rest of us
well,
bliss, simple bliss.

EMMA'S POEM

for Emma Louise Winer

Emma is joy
in blond hair and curls.

Bright smile at thirty-six months
steals my heart
with a single hug.

Emma is joy
in swim suit and red rubber boots

splashing in the pool, laughing.
"Ken, come here."

Of course.
I never could resist
those red boots.

Point Sur Lighthouse Station

I admire the
tenacity of a
dandelion growing

out of sheer rock,
feeding on ocean
mist.

I would
like to be so
trusting,

never knowing,
just blooming
wild and yellow.

FREELANCE WRITER FOR HIRE

I string words together for money, like popcorn
on a Christmas tree. It pays the bills,
like driving a cab. I took money from people
I didn't know to get them from here to there.

Sometimes they snorted coke or ate or smoked
joints in the back seat. Once they were having sex
on the way to the airport at three in the morning.

I sell words about things that don't matter.
The cab had a destination.
The words let me buy Joni Mitchell CD's.

THE STARRY NIGHT

is best described by
people who can't move
away from its swirls and
torrents, spires and hills,
violent, passionate strokes.

Feet glued to the floor,
some point and whisper,
some stare until their faces
melt into aqua blue waves
to hold Vincent's yellow sun.

People stroll past
Cezanne, Picasso
Diego Rivera.

Nobody passes here
without taking the time to
dwell in a small house
beneath blue hills.

SEVEN A.M. AT SHORELINE

Under a cacophony of circling swallows,
like a bees nest in motion, wild geese rise.
Mother earth has just shed a layer of brown skin –
a flying V honking its way over the water.

Snowy egret, graceful as morning mist
in the wind, stretches her long silky, white neck,
the pelicans, the ducks,
dance together on the glass-smooth bay.

Nearby, Silicon Valley goes to work
in square grey cubicles. CEOs fire up
spreadsheets. Suits and jeans with beepers
scurry to the next important meeting.

They don't taste the green, brown meadow
that ambles forward to meet the bay,
the great blue heron or the common sea gull.

There are no mistakes
in God's world. Eventually death
will claim us all.

The giant white pelican with
black tipped wings will continue
to rest on the water.

Unreasonable Expectations

You will go
to your mother's house.
You will eat

turkey and like it.
She will get drunk.
Nobody will say anything.

You will sit at the table
and drift off to the time
your father beat you.

You will smile
and say thank you
for the mashed potatoes.

You will sit or stand
around the piano
and sing.

You will miss
your girlfriend, who
doesn't love you anymore.

You will be grateful
for the two $20 bills
in the Christmas card

from Dad. You
will calculate $240
remembering Christmases past.

You will hug
your sister and smile
because you know you won't

see her again
until next year. You will
wonder about your favorite uncle

the one nobody talks about.
You will smile warmly
when you hand the red

wrapped box with a gold bow
to your four-year-old niece
who bit your hand last year.

You will smile
and laugh and hug everybody
goodbye and thank them for

such a wonderful Christmas.

TOTEM IN GREEN FATIGUES

The homeless man
in the yogurt shop
wanted someone to buy him
a frozen yogurt.
I wouldn't.
I don't know why.
He smelled bad.
He scared me.

Like a totem in green fatigues,
sad red eyes and scraggly beard,
he leaned against the pink wall
between posters of yogurt shakes
and fruit cups. He didn't speak.

We tried our best
to ignore him,
the way you might ignore
an elephant in your living room.

Many years ago
someone held a baby and tried
to imagine
what he might become.
Nobody holds the shadow.
Nobody looks at him.

LIFE IS GOOD

I spent my time in the garden this morning.
It's mine to spend.
God gave it to me.
I'm waiting for my tomatoes to turn red
for my peppers to get hot
carefully eyeing my zucchini
to see if it's going to take over the world.

Poetry and revolution before breakfast

– Edward Abbey

The Second Coming

1

The second coming arrived on Broadway and 42nd
Street just before New Years Eve. He stood
in his robe, scraggly beard and sandals,
appearing a little dazed, or maybe just ethereal.
He looked like he belonged there.

"Where is this place?" he asked
a passerby in Times Square.
"What!" said the incredulous man.
"Who the fuck are you?"
"Jesus," said the second coming.
"Hey," said the incredulous man, "no need to curse, but
you do look like him."
He directed the second coming to Madison Ave.

The second coming stepped out of a cab on Madison
a few blocks from Grand Central Station.
He had no money,
but even a New York City cab driver respects
a good miracle.
A sign said, "The J. Walter Thompson Agency."
The second coming entered.

Sitting before the man who would become his agent,
the second coming explained about God and Salvation
and Peace and how much God loves purple flowers.
The agent thought he was nuts.
But there was something compelling about this man
in his robe, scraggly beard and sandals,
appearing a little dazed, or maybe just ethereal.

"Maybe we should call the Pope," said the agent.
"Who?" asked the second coming.

"It's too complicated to explain.
Maybe we should call a news conference."

The agent called the New York Times
and the New York Post
and the Washington Post and the Daily News
and the National Enquirer, the American Spectator,
ABC, NBC, CBS, CNN, The Christian
Broadcasting Network,
the Christian Science Monitor,
various Web site providers,
the White House, and his mother.

The second coming and his agent stepped out of a cab
in front of St. Patrick's Cathedral (it was the agent's idea).
The second coming looked at the tall spired building.
The cross made him wince. He looked down at his feet,
rubbed his hands together, scratched his forehead.

"Where is this place," asked the second coming?
"St. Patrick's Cathedral," said the agent. "It's a church."
"A what?" "It's too complicated to explain."

It was a slow news day,
so lots of reporters came for the second coming.
They brought notebooks and tape recorders
and microphones on boom stands and cameras, satellite
uplinks technicians, toys and perfect haircuts.

The second coming stood on the steps of St. Patrick's
Cathedral. He explained about God and Salvation
and Peace and how much God loves purple flowers.

The reporters held their notebooks
like they were covering a stump speech,
but there was something compelling about this man
in his robe, scraggly beard and sandals,
appearing a little dazed, or maybe just ethereal.

"What's your position on abortion," someone asked?
"On what," asked the second coming?   "Baby killing,"
said the man from the Christian Broadcasting Network.
"It's a sin to kill babies."

And the headline read:
"The Second Coming Has Come, Condemns Abortion."
The agent was pleased with the coverage.
The second coming was confused.

An editorial in the New York Times cautioned.
The Christian Science Monitor applauded.
USA Today ran an eight-inch story with color charts of
Jerusalem and Bethlehem.
CNN tried to get him on Larry King Live.
Someone called the President.
Someone called the Vatican.

The agent booked a suite at the Trump Plaza.
The second coming preferred to sleep
with the homeless on a steam grate in front of Tiffany's. He
talked to the homeless of God and Salvation and Peace
and how much God loves purple flowers,
until a policeman rousted him and said
he couldn't sleep there. So he slept on a bench
in Central Park.

2

The second coming was not good news to the Vatican.
The Pope made oblique, noncommittal statements
about "this figure who has appeared"
and tried to keep his options open.
He worried.

The President weighed the political benefits
of embracing the second coming, and the possibility that
the second coming was a scam. He knew about scams.

The President ordered the FBI
to do a background check
on the second coming's agent and the CIA
to look for coded messages in his words
about God and Salvation and Peace
and how much God loves purple flowers.
He worried.

The Christian Coalition liked his stance
on abortion, and so
embraced him immediately. They printed millions
of voter guides with a check box for which candidates
supported the second coming and which ones did not.
They didn't worry. They felt righteous.

The media fumed because
the second coming didn't do interviews.
So they interviewed scholars and pundits,
rabbis and priests, monks and nuns,
and mother superiors. Peter Jennings walked
through virtual reality sets of Jerusalem and Bethlehem.
Geraldo called it "the greatest story since O.J."
Steven Bochco plotted the TV series.
The networks looked for sponsors.

Birkenstock brought out a new line of sandals
like the ones the second coming wore. Ralph Lauren
marketed a now familiar looking robe. Trendy students
and rock n' rollers grew scraggly beards
and hung out at Tower Records.
Kids went to school with second coming lunch boxes.
The agent collected royalties.
The second coming slept in Central Park
and attracted crowds.

3

The second coming made the agent nervous.
The agent experienced a spiritual awakening.
He started to spend more time in Central Park and less
time at second coming headquarters in his Plaza suite.
The agent still wore his blue suit, white shirt,
red tie and black shoes, but he thought of giving up his
cellular phone and his beeper.

The agent tried to get the second coming
to read The New York Times and watch CNN.
The second coming listened to the homeless
who came to hear him talk about God and Salvation
and Peace and how much God loves purple flowers.

4

The second coming's second news conference
drew reporters from around the world. They brought
notebooks and tape recorders and microphones on
boom stands and cameras, satellite uplinks technicians,
toys and perfect haircuts.
They snarled traffic all over Manhattan.

"Would you clarify your position on abortion,"
a reporter asked?
"I have no position on abortion,"
said the second coming.
"But it was reported that you said..."
"That was incorrect.
My agent will supply you with a transcript."
The second coming was no longer confused.

A Gnostic scholar asked,
"Can you put an end to speculation
that you had relations with Mary Magdalene?"
"Yes, I can," said the second coming.

The crowd leaned forward.
"Stop speculating."

"The Pope has refused to declare that
you are the legitimate second coming."
"Render unto the Pope what is the Pope's.
When he leaves his castle and gets down here
in the streets with the rest of us,
then he'll have an opinion worth considering."

Asked about welfare reform, he said:
"We should not turn our backs on the poor."
On the Middle East: "Those people
have never gotten along."
On Rwanda: "Feed the people and there will be peace."
On Ken Starr and Bill Clinton:
 "Father forgive them. They know not..."
On the Christian Coalition: "They're using my name
without my permission."
On premarital sex: "Is this something new?"
On homosexuality: "Is this something new?"
On the current state of the world:
"It's pretty much as I left it, just more crowded."
"Why have you come back?"
"Because it's time."
"Thank you for coming."
The second coming walked back to the park.
It started to rain. Nobody moved.

The New York Times headline read:
"Second Coming Slams Pope,
Supports Abortion Rights."
The National Star headline read:
"Jesus and Mary: The Inside Story,"
which was also the name of the NBC miniseries.

The second coming appeared on Oprah and Larry King,
Today Show and Good Morning America.

He skipped Jenny Jones.
He gave interviews to C-SPAN, the Wall Street Journal,
the New York Times, Wolf Blitzer and Dev Null. His
Web site, www.secondcoming.com, got more than
a million hits a week.

Planes landed at Kennedy Airport.
Thousands of people flocked to Central Park.
The networks worried about ratings.
The mayor worried about crowd control.
The President worried about his image.
The Pope worried about his power.
He called the President on a secure line.
The Christian Coalition was pissed.
They printed new voter guides.

5

Just before Christmas the stores were empty.
Toys stayed on the shelves.
Expensive jewelry stayed in its case.
Nobody bought gift certificates
for McDonald's Happy Meals.
The churches were cavernous.

Nobody rode elevators, sat at desks, made important
phone calls, sent faxes or e-mail, negotiated deals,
underwrote offerings, invested in the internet,
speculated about the future of Apple Computer,
shopped at Safeway, cleaned the executive bathroom,
reviewed the R&D budget, tweaked the distribution
system, downsized, upsized or rightsized.

The Conference Board reported
Consumer Confidence was at an all-time high.
Consumer Spending was at an all-time low.
The economy neared collapse.
The second coming taught from his bench in Central

Park in his robe, scraggly beard and sandals
appearing a little dazed, or maybe just ethereal.
He fed the masses.

6

The President never mentioned the second coming by
name. He didn't appear to be concerned.
Neither did prime ministers, monarchs, bishops
and the Christian Coalition,
who held secret teleconferences on secured lines.

7

The second coming knew the day had come.
He did nothing different.
His hands started to bleed. His feet hurt. He got
headaches.
His side ached.
He said nothing.

The second coming sat in silent contemplation
before a crowd of half-a-million. Everybody prayed
and munched on manna.

The second coming barely noticed
the glint in the tree.
He turned to face God.
It was like slow motion–
the bullet coming towards him.
He spread his arms,
looked toward Home.
"Insanity," he thought, "is doing the same thing
over and over
and expecting different results."
"God, my God," he said,
"why does this keep happening to me?"